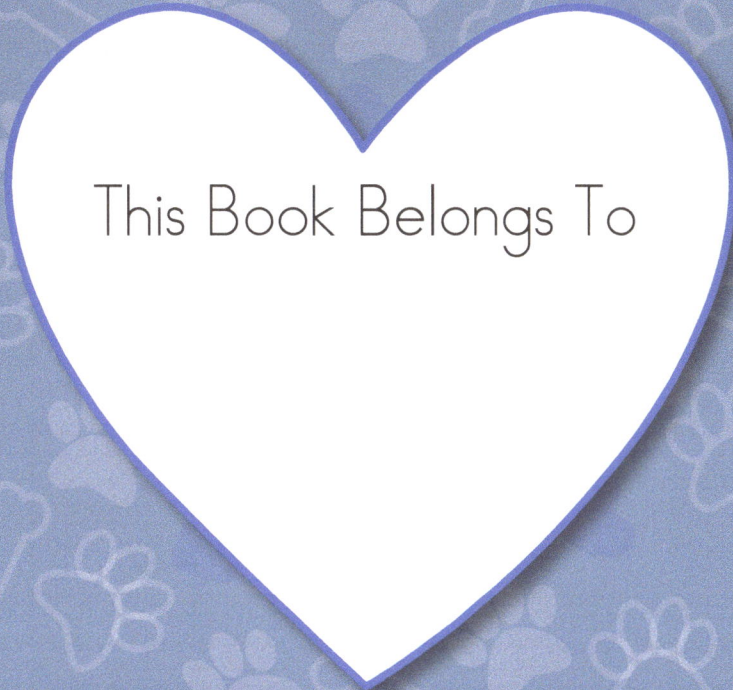

This Book Belongs To

# The Story About Tigger And Elsa

by Cameron Pendergraft

Illustrated by Jennifer Tipton Cappoen

**Author:** Cameron Pendergraft
**Cover Designer and Illustrator:** Jennifer Tipton Cappoen
**Editor:** Lynn Bemer Coble

**PCKids** is an imprint of **Paws and Claws Publishing, LLC.**
1589 Skeet Club Road, Suite 102 #175
High Point, NC 27265
www.PawsandClawsPublishing.com
info@pawsandclawspublishing.com


ISBN # 978-1-946198-15-0
Printed in the United States

To my children.

Tigger was a funny-looking dog. She had soft, little ears. She had short, sturdy legs and a long, chubby body. She had kind-looking eyes that were the warm-brown color of chocolate.

Tigger's first family left her at an animal shelter when they moved. Tigger lived there for seven long and lonely months.

Eventually the happy day came when Tigger was chosen to be adopted! Her new adoptive family loved to rub her soft, little ears. They loved to gaze into her beautiful brown eyes that were the color of chocolate. They thought her short, sturdy legs and long, chubby body helped make her the prettiest dog in the world.

Tigger was happy. She had a soft couch on which to sleep. She had squeaky toys with which to play. She always had plenty of food and water to eat and drink. She had everything she wanted and needed.

But the family she loved wanted her to have one more thing. They thought something was missing in Tigger's life. They wanted her to have a playmate.

And so back to the animal shelter they went. They started the search for just the right companion for their dear Tigger.

Tigger's family knew she liked to play tug-of-war with her squeaky toys, so this new addition had to be playful.

Tigger's favorite game was being sprayed with a garden hose. She ran excitedly through the water sprinkler. This new pup had to love water play too!

Tigger enjoyed the family's daily walks through the woods. She was happy pouncing in the sticks and leaves. She loved to roll in the grass.

Any new addition to
her family had to be
able to run alongside
Tigger. The new
dog had to be
able to keep
up on these
walks.

One quiet afternoon, her family placed a little, bright-white fluff of a dog beside Tigger on her bed. When Tigger tried to sniff the pup, she felt a snap and heard a yap!

*What was that?* Tigger's big eyes asked her family.

"Tigger, this is your new sister. Her name is Elsa. She needs a family. She may *look* a bit different. But we promise you she can do everything you can do."

Elsa scampered away from Tigger. She tiptoed across the floor to a water bowl. At that moment, Tigger noticed that Elsa was *not* exactly like her. This bright-white fluff of a pup only had three legs!

Tigger wondered to herself: *Could this little white fluff of a thing play tug-of-war with squeaky toys? Would*

she be able to chase the water stream from the garden hose? Could Elsa keep up with her on long walks through the woods with only three little legs? Tigger wasn't so sure.

The first day of life with Elsa was interesting. Tigger let Elsa sniff and play with all her toys. But when she tried to join in, Elsa snapped and yapped at her. Tigger just put her head down, hung out her tongue, and let out a deep sigh.

Tigger had a feeling that playing with Elsa might not turn out to be much fun after all.

Tigger led Elsa to her bowl of dog kibble and stood back to give Elsa room to eat. When Elsa finished, she turned toward Tigger. Elsa snapped, yapped, and then hopped away.

Tigger wasn't at all sure how she felt about this pup.

When it was time for Tigger's daily walk in the woods, she was excited to have Elsa tag along. Tigger took off to lead the way. However, Elsa had no problem speeding right past Tigger with only her three little legs!

During her daily walks in the woods, Tigger's treats were meat bits. But Tigger noticed that Elsa was being tossed pieces of a carrot.

*Was this bright-white, fluffy thing a bunny? Had her family of people who loved her gotten her a bunny instead of a dog? Surely not!*

Later that very day, friends and family members stopped by to see the new, little bright-white puppy with three legs. Folks oohed and aahed at the pretty puppy. In turn, Elsa snapped and yapped at each new face.

Tigger heard the people speak.

"What a pretty, little white puppy."

"You found her at the shelter?"

"Do you know how she lost her leg?"

Sweet Tigger wished she could let these people know how she felt about this snapping, yapping pup. And yet Tigger remembered well how scared and unsure she had been when she first came to live with this family of people that she now loved.

Tigger never snapped or yapped. But it did take her a while to learn to trust the family who had chosen her. And now they had chosen Elsa.

*Things had to get better. But when?*

That night when Tigger headed over to her dog bed to go to sleep for the night, she found Elsa there. The pup was sound asleep. Tigger didn't mind.

She just lay on the floor right beside the dog bed, let out a deep sigh, and fell asleep. Tigger was happy not to have heard yet another yap from Elsa. She was glad Elsa didn't snap at her.

The next day the two dogs headed out with their family for their daily walk through the woods. Elsa led the way. Tigger ran to keep up, because she was excited about getting her meat treats. Surely Elsa would beat her, and Elsa would get her carrot treats first.

But when Tigger got to where she thought she would catch up to Elsa, Elsa wasn't there! Tigger barked. Then she waited.

*Where was Elsa?*

Elsa was called. "Elsa, ...!"

Then Tigger heard the familiar, "Yap. Yap. Yap!"

Tigger took off at full speed. She knew those yaps were coming from the pond down the hill that they passed every day on their walk.

Sure enough, Tigger found Elsa there. She was in the water stuck under a log. The pup must have seen a hopping frog and chased it into the pond. Tigger had chased many a frog into that pond.

But the thick mud at the bottom of the pond wasn't too deep for Tigger's strong legs. Elsa was small and had only *three* legs to push herself free.

With only one back leg, she was trapped in the mud. Poor little Elsa was yapping and shaking from head to paw all at the same time.

YAP

YAP

YAP

YAP

YAP

"Tigger, can you help Elsa?"

Tigger knew what she had to do. She waded into the muddy pond. She pushed the log that was holding Elsa over and away with her big strong head and her strong sturdy legs.

Then she pushed little Elsa to the water's edge with her strong head. Elsa rushed to the edge of the pond and ran up into the long grass to shake and bark.

She yapped a happy yap and licked Tigger's face. She was glad to be free.

WAS TIGGER HER HERO?

Tigger walked into the long grass to roll and roll and dry off. Elsa rolled down into the grass beside Tigger and did the same.

When they sat up to lick themselves clean, Elsa gently placed a paw on Tigger's leg.

"Tigger, I think you've made a forever friend, Girl. Oh, sweet Tigger."

Then Tigger and Elsa stood up and pranced side by side all the way back home.

That night Tigger and Elsa fell asleep side by side in Tigger's comfy bed. Elsa didn't move over all night, even when Tigger's snoring got loud!

The next morning, the two dogs shared a bowl of kibble. Afterward Elsa pulled out all of Tigger's squeaky toys. She spread them out on the kitchen floor. The dogs tussled and pulled at the toys together. Maybe Elsa had finally learned to trust Tigger.

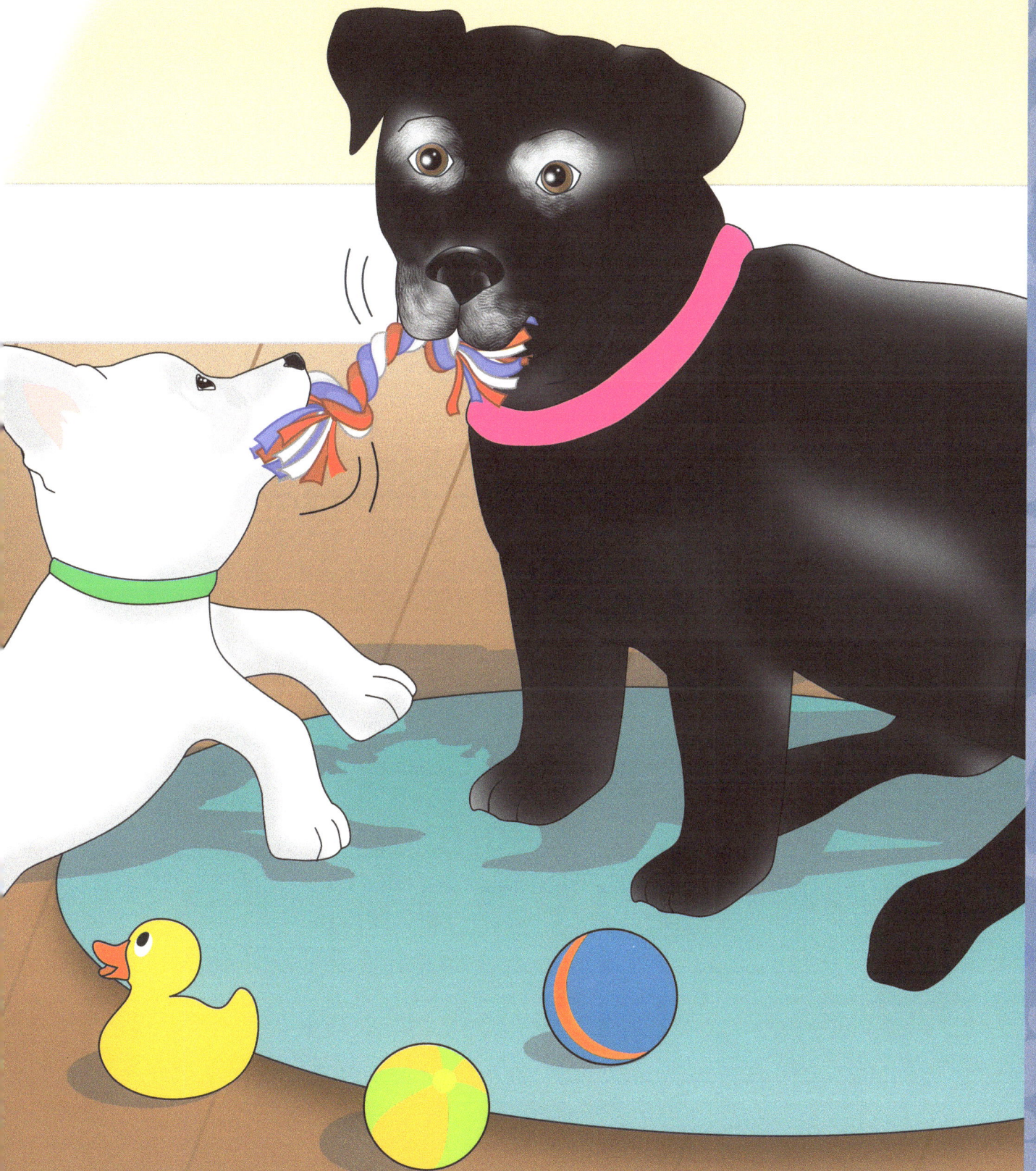

When they headed out for their morning walk, Tigger made sure Elsa stayed up front so she could keep a watchful eye on her frisky, new little sister. The little white ball of fluff may have had only three legs. She may have liked to yap and snap to be heard and seen.

But Tigger knew one thing for sure:

Elsa was an important part of the family of people that Tigger loved. Tigger would always make sure Elsa knew they all loved her.

Tigger watched Elsa run and stop. Then she flipped and pounced through the tall grass.

*Surely Elsa was smart enough not to chase another hopping frog into the muddy pond.*

Elsa raced toward the pond. Then she backed away and yapped. She hurried to Tigger's side. Tigger gave Elsa's head a lick.

Then they turned back toward home. The two dogs pranced side by side, back toward the house of people that they loved.

The house Tigger—and now Elsa—called home.

HOME SWEET HOME

# About the Author

Cameron lives in Oxford, North Carolina, with her husband Steve, their dogs Tigger and Elsa, and three cats.

*The Story About Tigger and Elsa* is her second children's book.

Cameron and Elsa

Cameron and Tigger